Nurture
My Heart

A Nurtured Heart Approach™ Handbook

Igniting the Greatness in Every Child

Catherine Stafford, LCSW

Catherine Stafford lives with her husband and four children outside of Seattle, Washington. She is a Licensed Clinical Social Worker in private practice and a certified Nurtured Heart Approach specialist. Contact the author directly for speaking, coaching or counseling services at www.nurturemyheart.com

Other books by this author:

• Teacher, Nurture My Heart—Igniting the Greatness in Every Student
• Your Greatness is Growing—Nurturing the Heart of Autism

Nurture My Heart: A Nurtured Heart Approach Handbook

Written and illustrated by Catherine Stafford, LCSW

Layout and design by Mark Kunzelmann

ISBN 978-0-9838610-1-0
Publisher: Greatness Grows Publications, Snohomish, Washington

Printed in the United States of America

"Nurture My Heart" is dedicated to ...

my Emma, Ben, Luke and Jack who continue to grow and shine in their greatness every day. To my husband Brian, who embodies the quality of positivity with his endless support of my projects. With deepest gratitude to Howard Glasser, creator of the Nurtured Heart Approach for creating this work that has enriched my life.

For more information on the Nurtured Heart Approach, please visit www.childrenssuccessfoundation.com

Dear Parent,

Nurture My Heart is intended for any parent or adult who desires a powerful yet simple formula for growing greatness in children. It is a formula for creating a family or classroom culture based on genuine success and positive relationship.

Nurture My Heart is a story and summary of Howard Glasser's Nurtured Heart Approach™, presented in a way that provides a tool to introduce the approach to children and a concise explanation of the basics of the approach.

Why not start with success? Conventional parenting relies on our cultural tendency to spend most of our time and energy answering the question, "what's wrong with this picture?" so a child is spoken to and recognized more frequently and more energetically when misbehaving. The unintended outcome is a child with a negative sense of self, who acts from this place of negativity, feels bad on the inside, and knows only what he is not.

Howard Glasser's Nurtured Heart Approach reverses this unintended outcome. It shows parents how to answer the question, in exquisite detail, "what's right with my child?"

Parents learn how to recognize and celebrate a child for making good choices, and they master the skills to build within their children all of the values and character qualities that create a healthy sense of self and ownership in creating one's successful future: inner wealth!

Nurture My Heart demonstrates how simple it is to start with success and forever maintain a positive, strong relationship with your average or intense, uniquely amazing child. As a mother of four children and as a therapist, I have found the Nurtured Heart Approach to be a profoundly transformational philosophy. I wish you every success and renewed passion for parenting as you open your heart to the journey that lies ahead.

To the greatness that is in every child!

— Catherine Stafford, Author

Today is a beginning: a fresh clean start.
The words that I share
will come straight from my heart.

My goal is to show you
in ways that are straight,
the undeniable truth of the many
ways that you're great.

My words may sound silly,
but they are honest and true.
They are meant to reflect greatness
that I see in you.

It is not about noticing problems and messes.
My focus is set on creating successes.

Integrity, humor, helpful intentions
are qualities I will honor
and enthusiastically mention.

Each rule that you follow,
great character I see,
will be met with reflections of
your great choices from me.

"I see that you
are up out of bed
and not late."

"You tried all of your dinner
and never used the word 'hate'."

"You just helped your sister
with the worry that she had.
That shows great awareness
to sense she was sad."

"I love that you are following
the no shouting rule.
You have self-control when you're frustrated
and can still keep your cool."

Sometimes I may slip up
and not stay firm in my stands.
I may occasionally nag,
stomp or throw up my hands.

But, you stopped in your tracks
when I told you to wait.
"Wow! That's respectful and patient.
Those qualities are so great."

When I say that's a "reset"
(for a rule that you break),
during the calming
breaths that you take...

Remember, "it's just a reset",
a short break, a re-take.

"Great Self-control."

I'm not angry, I won't lecture;
the moment has passed.
I intend to grow greatness
in ways that will last.

If you lose track of time
and you get home a bit late,
we will take it in stride;
it doesn't change how you're great.

Greatness may feel new,
but it's the core truth renewed.
I will nurture your heart
as a gift of love to you.

We will practice a lot,
talking much of successes.
These moments define you,
not broken rules, slips or messes.

Life is about learning;
we can always rewind.
We can make up for mistakes,
like being unkind.

It's what you feel inside that's important;
the good you know about you.
I am making a promise to help you feel it too.

Growing greatness of self
is called inner wealth.
It is a critical part of your overall health.

Let's work together on this:
each moment a fresh start.
Remember, my words will
come straight from my heart.

With focused attention,
this will be a great day!
You are a GREAT kid in so many ways!

Building Inner Wealth in Our Children

"Children need to be strong on the inside, now more than ever before." — Howard Glasser

The Nurtured Heart Approach™ is a simple and powerful conceptual framework and set of specific techniques that was created to shift even the most intense children into a pattern of recurrent and irrefutable success. It is about actively guiding children back to their truest self; relentlessly realigning children with who they are at their very core. With the Nurtured Heart Approach as their guide, adults proactively grow great character and behavior by describing, in specific detail, all of the positive choices that are observed, in everyday moments, as they are occurring. It is this present moment focus that creates powerful internalized success for even the most intense children. By focusing on present moment success, positive relationship and teaching social learning contextually, children redefine themselves and shift into a trajectory of internalized success ... greatness. When we shine the light on the successes that we create, even in seemingly insignificant moments, children begin to live out their greatness. We create what we see, simply by tuning in to it and giving it our full attention and appreciation. Beautiful life force energy, once viewed as challenging, propels children into a trajectory of internal (and external) success. Children and families are transformed and the best news is that the parent, grandparent, caregiver or educator gets to be the hero of this story by awakening children to the greatness inside.

The beauty of the Nurtured Heart Approach is its ability to reach far beyond improvement to the glorious place of lasting and internalized transformation. The outcome of focused adult energy is an internal shift in how a child defines himself and his future. As children develop and begin to trust this new inner compass through expanding inner wealth, not only will they be able to tackle life's challenges, but they will be inspired to live their lives in greater and more substantial ways. Inner wealth, as described in *All Children Flourishing* by Howard Glasser, is a child's growing and deepening sense of:

- Optimism
- Being Lovable
- Having much to give
- Being filled with life force—and not being afraid of it
- Being open to, less afraid of, and non-resistant to change
- Being excited about the prospects of life and of living life fully
- Being able to handle strong feelings
- Being unafraid of intimacy
- Being less likely to be consumed by anxiety, stress and depression
- Being better connected to one's body— and taking better care of it.

- Wonder and awe
- Trust and faith
- Holding great intentions
- Loving life, self & others
- Seeing what is true and living in truthfulness
- Having ready access to the "inner compass" that guides intuition
- Being present to self and others, in the moment
- Being in true power of body, heart and soul
- Having the courage to create, express and adapt to whatever is next
- Happiness in everyday life—no need for thrill-seeking
- Caring deeply for all life on the planet
- Seeing beauty in nature, art, the universe & life
- Moving away from addictive patterns
- Taking responsibility for contributions to the world—by way of choices
- Being appreciative, grateful and forgiving
- Being principled and making honorable decisions
- Using excellent judgment and making intelligent decisions
- Being respectful
- Being reverent
- Living in one's heart
- Believing in and inspired to live one's greatness

When children begin to experience growing inner wealth, they feel good about themselves; confident in their own skills and character. They begin to take control of their power and intensity. The more they experience success, the more they see themselves as successful. The more they use their intensity in healthy and powerful ways, the more confidence they have for making wise choices. Children in tune with their growing inner wealth begin to trust themselves and their ability to be successful. Children make better choices; accept responsibility, experience confidence in themselves and their ability to create their own bright future. This is the transformation that comes through the Nurtured Heart Approach and it is a beautiful and more inspiring journey for all. The process of learning, living and supporting children's growth through the Nurtured Heart Approach is the adult's journey. Children just come along for the ride, as significant adults shift their intention to positive relationship, great boundaries, refusing to energize the negative, and relentlessly creating true moments of success.

Key Concepts for the Nurtured Heart Approach

At the core of the **Nurtured Heart Approach** are several key concepts that frame the approach's transformational power.

These concepts are grounded in the energetic truth that intense children are drawn to significant adults' most excited and animated interactions, their energy, regardless of the content of those moments. Intensity seeks intensity.

Concept No 1: You are your child's favorite toy (Toys R Us)

Children seek relationship and they will follow the energetic flow to the most exciting connection. As a teacher or parent, your animation, dynamic interaction and energy (relationship) is the prize that a child is seeking to access. While this is often a subconscious process, children are paying keen attention and know just how to get the most exciting bells and whistles going. For many intense children, adults are more dynamic and alive in relation to negativity or misbehavior. Even with loving intention, this problem focused attention is steeped in secondary gain and proves too compelling for intense children. It is critical for significant adults to astutely observe and reflect on when they are more alive and present. Children equate adults' enthusiasm and energy to what they love. Picture how the football dad responds to the winning touchdown. By jumping up and down and yelling at the TV, dad sends a clear message of his passion for football. Be mindful to turn your energetic switch to "off" when a child is breaking rules or misbehaving and to "high" when a child demonstrates positive behavior and character. An intense child will feel more celebrated and appreciated for negative behavior if misbehavior brings the most animated and interactive engagement. This does not mean that parents ever should ignore negative behaviors, simply that they do not solicit the most exciting responses. Each and every interaction with a child sends a message of what is valued and appreciated. Being mindful of this fact, places adults in a position of great influence over how a child defines his relationship with the world.

> NOTE: *For some children, like those with more severe Autism, you may not feel like you are your child's favorite toy. In this case, the adult's job is to become that most valued prize, wooing the child through energetic, child focused attention, centered on the child's interests and abilities. Be the prize!*

Concept No 2: Creating success that would not otherwise exist (Shamu)

Key to Nurtured Heart Approach parenting is honoring a child's effort to make good choices, act responsibly and demonstrate good character. Each moment with a child has the opportunity to send a message of failure or one of success. Intense children have a strong experiential history of secondary gain from misbehavior. When adults purposefully notice and honor all effort toward a desired behavior, we provide the energetic momentum to encourage a child down the path of success. It is this firsthand experience of success and feeling appreciated that is the jet fuel for transformation to occur. Just as Shamu's trainers celebrated each step toward his mighty leaps over the high rope, we celebrate each step in a child's journey toward mighty achievement or desired goals. This does not mean lowering standards, but rather creating success around intentional movement in the desired direction. As Howard Glasser likes to say, "take a molecule and make it a miracle."

Concept No 3: Everything is subject to interpretation (Story of the Toll Booth Attendant)

Just as a toll booth attendant can see the beauty, autonomy and creative freedom throughout his day, if he so chooses, so too can adults choose to see what is right and worthy of appreciation in each opportunity-filled moment. When we look through a lens of radical appreciation and positivity, we begin see the beauty of successes previously overlooked. Instead of "what's wrong with this picture?" commit to seeking and energizing what is going right in each moment. What we call out in our children, what we accuse them of, will magnify before our eyes. Choose to see the greatness!

Concept No 4: What a child needs for life to make sense (Video Game Analogy)

Adults often wonder why a child can spend countless hours focused on video games, but be unable to sit through a meal or clean their room. When a child is playing a video game, life (inside the game) makes total sense. There is clarity around rules and when rules are followed the bells sound and points are accumulating; success is clear. When rules are broken, there is a brief interruption (a consequence) and then the child is right back into the game of success. Success becomes unavoidable and achieving success becomes the driving force. Video games are compelling because of this clarity and default to success; no matter what the child does, the game puts him right back on to the success track. Success, with effort, becomes unavoidable. As in a video game, Nurtured Heart Approach parents learn to provide clarity of rules, no energy for the negative and a default to success. Life makes total sense.

Concept No 5: Portfolio

Every significant adult interaction with a child helps to shape that child's developing sense of self and creates an opportunity for an energetic message to be downloaded. With traditional parenting, even "positive parenting," parents are much more alive and present when children misbehave. Messages laced with lectures and negativity, warnings and even pep-talks create downloads of failure; how the child did not measure up, messed up again, disappointed or fell short. All children, and particularly intense children, internalize these failures in a way that creates a negative sense of self; children who know very well what qualities they are not. Challenging children operate from this place of negativity, internalizing these adult interactions as a reflection of who they really are and knowing that negativity is the best pathway to intense relationship. Through the Nurtured Heart Approach, we relentlessly pursue a child's heart, seeking to realign him with his greatest version of himself. The greatness is already there, waiting to be re-awakened through firsthand experiences of the successes that challenge a negative portfolio. When we accuse children of great character and great choices, in the moment that they are occurring, children begin to have the evidence to challenge this negative sense of self. When we arm children with evidence, through the power of positivity and success, children begin to redefine themselves, based on the irrefutable truth of present moment evidence of who they truly are at their core. They begin to stand in their greatness, stepping onto the path of transformation.

NOTE: *All children are in the process of developing their sense of self, regardless of challenges or diagnosis. It is critical that adults nurture the growth of desired social learning skills through creating moments of success; relentlessly and tenaciously creating success. This not only leads to a more positive sense of self, but also greater sustainability and generalizability of new skills.*

The Three Stands

The foundation of the **Nurtured Heart Approach** is the Three Stands.

Think of the three stands as a three-legged stool; each leg balances the other. The stool will not stand if one of the three legs is not in firmly in place. Typical parenting backfires with intense children, because the relationship intensity occurs in relation to misbehavior. The Nurtured Heart Approach is not about learning yet another new way to control behavior. In fact, it is just the opposite. It is about learning a philosophy that celebrates success in such a way the negativity no longer holds value. It is the intentional relinquishing of adult effort to control children's behavior. With Nurtured Heart Approach we give in to the truth, that despite our best efforts, the only one who can control a child's behavior and emotions is that child. We take the three stands to guide the process of a child owning this control in healthy and powerful ways.

Stand 1: Refuse to give more energy to the negative

Resolve to not get drawn in to giving the child greater response, animation, or other unintended payoffs for misbehavior. Avoid, at all costs, accidentally fostering failures and rewarding problems with your energy, animated reaction and relationship. This is what is called leaking negativity and in undermines the effectiveness of the approach by defusing the solidity of the child's emerging inner wealth. The message must be made clear that the pathway to intense relationship does not flow through negativity. This is accomplished only by example. A child must live this fact experientially.

The Nurtured Heart Approach is about grace and this applies to the adults too. When you slip up, just catch yourself and move on to the next opportunity filled moment.

Stand 2: The relentless pursuit and celebration of success

Resolve to 1) purposefully create and nurture present moment successes, 2) relentlessly and strategically draw children into new and renewed patterns of success, and 3) live "in the moment" and shine the light on success in each moment. This is the power to change lives. It is through the active creation of success that we challenge how a child perceives himself at his very core. We do not wait to "catch a child being good," but rather we purposefully and strategically create an irrefutable string of successes that even the most intense and negative child cannot deny. This is where we begin to observe the new definition of self emerging, through growing inner wealth.

Stand 3: Clarity of Rules

Resolve to have: 1) clear rules and 2) clear, consistent and effective consequences when the rules are broken. There are two parts to this stand. The first is that rules are stated in extremely clear language ("No" language) so that a child knows exactly where the line is between rule followed and rules broken. Rules are about what a child should NOT do. You can build inner wealth and a wonderful sense of success when you give positive reflections whenever a child is NOT breaking a rule.

The second part of strict rule enforcement is committing always to deliver a consequence when a rule is broken: no warnings, negotiations, lectures or "you better stop that" looks. Consequences must be clear, predictable and consistent. By providing this clarity, delivered with neutrality, we help a child redefine his relationship with rules. Breaking rules no longer holds any value, as there is nothing to be gained.

Always follow through! Teach rules through enforcing a consequence when rules are broken and celebrating and energizing when rules are not being broken. By energizing both ends of the spectrum (rules being followed and rules not broken) we expand the continuum for creating success. Success is unavoidable!

Recognitions/Reflections: Techniques to Support the Stands

It is time to move beyond the generic praise of "good job."

Recognitions are the pathway to nurture a child's heart, due to the specificity and enthusiasm the parent uses to reflect a child's greatness. It is through this passageway that we are able to speak directly to the heart and soul of a child with the truth of who they really are. We give our full attention and verbally recognize what a child is choosing to do right and not doing wrong, so that they feel seen and appreciated for their effort and good choices. We call this "energizing success."

When giving Active, Experiential, Proactive and Creative Recognitions, do not be afraid to use the big, powerful and "juicy" words. Children love to feel that they are worthy of thoughtful and powerful words. They will show you their ability to absorb the meaning and intent, through their own expanding vocabulary, as they demonstrate their own expanding inner wealth.

■ Active Recognition (Kodak):

Clearly observing what a child is doing, without any evaluation or judgment, just detailed observation; you say what you see. Simply taking a verbal snapshot of what a child is doing in any given moment. The result is that a child feels seen, acknowledged and appreciated, whether engaging in ordinary or exemplary behavior. This allows a parent or teacher to help a child feel loved and cherished just they way he is. There is no need to act out to extract adult energy or connection. The Active Recognition is the launch pad for the other techniques and the starting point for establishing the new language of success. We only use Active Recognitions when a child is not breaking a rule. Beginning an Active Recognition with "I see," "it looks like" or "I'm noticing" is a great way to keep reflections focused on the snapshot of the moment. Make the language your own, authentic to your style and personality.

EXAMPLES:

"I see that you are drawing your design with all sorts of colors and shapes. I see red and green and wavy lines."

"You are bouncy and look very excited to go outside to play."

"Check you out! You are really taking your time lacing your shoes just right."

....

You can use Active Recognitions before a rule is broken. By providing a reflection before a rule is broken, the momentum of a moment can often be shifted back towards good choices and success. If a child is struggling to make a good choice, this reflection is often enough to support a successful outcome. Adults can provide reflection of effort and offer support in the moment, before a rule is broken. The implication is one of expected success!

EXAMPLES:

"You look really bored and seem to be trying to figure out what you are going to do next."

"It looks like you are thinking about how to respond to the fact that Joe is in your spot."

"You two are clearly trying to figure out who gets to go first. Let me know if you need some help making a plan."

....

Use Active Recognitions to support healthy expression of emotion. It is critical that a child experience the success of working through the range of emotions. Learning how to regulate all emotions is essential to healthy development. An adult's tendency is to attempt to stop a child from feeling strong emotions, because it is appears uncomfortable or precipitates challenging behavior, or because it creates our own strong emotion in response. However, every time a child perceives that he is wrong for having an emotional response to a situation, through adult negative feedback, he becomes further removed from his feelings. It is only by the successful navigation through the range of emotions that a child will learn to trust his emotions as a strong and trustworthy internal compass for navigating life. Turn these moments of strong emotions into a moment of success. The adult goal is not to stop the emotion, but rather to name it and create success around it. When we name an emotion contextually, a child feels validated and honored. This is the pathway to growth in the ability to own all emotions in healthy ways. Often we can prevent a challenging behavior from occurring by simply honoring what a child is feeling.

EXAMPLES:

"I can see that you are disappointed by my answer."

"You look really sad that Joe picked Carl first. You are being powerful by feeling that feeling and still getting into the game."

"You look frustrated that your toy is not working. You are being strong right now by how you are handling that feeling."

NOTE: *There is always an emotion before a behavior. When we honor all emotions as necessary and valuable, we help children be less fearful of emotions and learn more adaptive ways to express emotion than through negativity and challenging behavior. Remember, what adults often label as anger (the behavioral manifestation of an emotion) is often the underlying emotion of frustration, disappointment or worry. Children feel validated by the correct labeling of an emotion. Move beyond mad, sad, happy when labeling emotions.*

....

Use Active Recognition to reflect the "communicative intent" of a behavior. For young children who have yet to develop a social skills repertoire, and children with social cognitive challenges, a behavior often serves a communicative purpose. As long as a rule is not being broken, use Active Recognitions in the moment to support learning and social success. Children with social communication challenges or language difficulties will use behavior to convey meaning when they do not have the language or emotional regulation skills to express their needs.

EXAMPLES:

"I see that you are standing close to me and trying to get my attention."

"It looks like you are looking at Johnny because you are thinking about playing with him."

"You are stomping your foot, which lets me know that you don't like my plan."

By adding a more adaptive behavioral choice, adults provide the scaffolding to creating a contextual moment of social success.

EXAMPLES:

"I see that you are standing close to me and trying to get my attention. You could tap my leg or say 'excuse me' and that lets me know you need my help."

"It looks like you are looking at Johnny because you are thinking about playing with him. You could ask Johnny if he wants to play cars or hand him one to let him know you want to play."

"You are stomping your foot because you don't like my plan. You can tell me 'I'm disappointed' or tell me your idea."

When adults label the communicative intent of a behavior, before a rule is broken, children feel understood and will not need to turn to less desirable alternatives for having their needs met. Do adults always know the communicative intent? Of course not, but make a educated guess and be sure that the child will let you know if your guess was accurate or not.

....

■ Experiential Recognitions (Polaroid):

Teaching values and character experientially, by using positive reflections to create a picture of how a current or recent event is a reflection of a desired character or value already present in that child. Experiential Recognitions are the pathway to the heart and soul of a child, proof positive of the greatness that is within. The reflection begins with a description of what was observed and then expands to the heart level by describing what that moment says about the child. Start with an Active Recognition and add a comment about how what the child is doing is a reflection of a value or great character. It is through these Experiential Recognitions that the shift begins in a child's portfolio. This is the pathway to standing in greatness.

EXAMPLES:

"The way that you just answered my question without stomping or yelling was a demonstration of respect and self-control."

"I just noticed that you helped your sister with her shoelaces. Thinking of her and offering support really shows how thoughtful and helpful you are."

"You grabbed the groceries without being asked. You are sure thinking ahead by knowing I would need help. What a team player!"

....

Use Experiential Recognitions to create moments of contextual social learning. It is not uncommon for intense young children, or children with social cognitive challenges, to be unsuccessful with their peers, due to underdeveloped social thinking/social skills. Children who spend their early years as the energetic "live wire" in the classroom are unavailable for social learning. Use Experiential Recognitions to provide experiential teaching opportunities to create social success. Begin with an Active Recognition, add the Experiential Recognition to create the success.

EXAMPLES:

"It looks like you want to ask Sally to play with you. I love how you are standing next to her and asked her to play with a friendly voice.

That really shows thoughtfulness and interest in a friend."

"When you played Legos with Joe you were really thinking of him. Playing a game that someone else chooses is really being a great friend."

Add a teaching moment if necessary to expand on the missing skill.

EXAMPLE:

"It looks like you want to ask Sally to play. I love how patient you are being by standing so quietly in front of her. You could ask 'do you want to play in the kitchen' and see what she says."

There are abundant Experiential Recognition opportunities proactively to teach the very behaviors, values and character that we want to grow in children. Make the commitment to apply this technique in the moments when a child is doing well; those moments when tempted to tip-toe past the door in an effort to not spoil the moment.

Think energetic, specific and positive! For an extra boost and to really drive the message to the heart level, add an additional statement about how the quality observed is one of greatness.

EXAMPLE:

"I want to let you know that the fact that you took responsibility is a sign of integrity and is a quality of greatness that I see in you."

■ Proactive Recognition (Canon):

Celebrating children for NOT breaking rules. By viewing rule-breaking as a matter of choice rather than a mistake, we can celebrate and pursue success in moments when rules are being followed or not being broken. Clarity around rule expectations through energizing success provides a constant flow of positive energy for rule following. Rule following becomes the compelling force. There is no need to discuss or post rules when rules are reinforced through success. This flow allows adults the freedom to create new rules as necessary. Be mindful only to create rules that you expect to reinforce and that all adults involved will support.

EXAMPLES:

"I love how you got out of the car and grabbed my hand right away. That is a great way to follow the rules for being safe in the parking lot."

"I could tell you were frustrated that Joey took your toy and you were really powerful by not hitting. You are so great at managing your emotions and following the rules to keep everyone safe."

"Wow, you are sitting in your chair and eating quietly with your fork! Way to follow the dinnertime rules."

"Now that you are 5, I want to tell you the new rule about shopping carts at the store."

Assume that a child is going to follow rules and begin to energize success at the very first opportunity.

EXAMPLE:

"Wow, we just got to the store and you are already following the rules of no running and no asking for candy. You are amazing at following rules and such a pleasure to shop with."

Use Proactive Recognitions liberally, enthusiastically and honestly. Remember to stay in the moment. Even if a child has recently broken a rule, the truth of the moment is reflected in the good choices being made currently. There are countless opportunities for Proactive Recognitions. Rules do not need to be something to be feared, but rather something to be celebrated.

....

■ Creative Recognitions:

Hijacking children into success; creating situations that transport even especially challenging children into success while promoting any child's sense of cooperation and collaboration. By creating compliance before a child can do otherwise, we create success that would not otherwise happen. Often when a child is given a directive, it is done so with the suggestion of an option. "Would you please take your shoes off and take them upstairs" implies a choice and the intense child will often choose "not now" as a way to retain his sense of control. Instead, begin a directive with "I need you to..." or "right now your job is to..." Statements like, "I would like you to do your homework" implies that the adult is simply giving an opinion, which the child may legitimately disagree with and choose not to do the homework. They child may not like to. "Your job is to get your backpack and start your homework" provides greater clarity and opportunities to begin to energize success.

EXAMPLE:

"I need you to take your shoes upstairs right now" is a guaranteed pathway to increased compliance. The moment that the child makes a move, begin to energize the success, "wow, I love how respectful you are by following directions right away."

Keep a directive a directive and save your own adult great manners for reflecting gratitude for compliance. They are more meaningful wrapped around creating a moment of success.

EXAMPLE:

"Thank you so much for being such a great listener and following my direction. You have the greatness of respect and helpfulness."

....

Nurtured Heart Reset (A radically different time-out)

One of the key concepts of the **Nurtured Heart Approach** is the notion that power is not in punishment.

Setting a child on to the new trajectory of success is not achieved through finding just the right punishment, but rather through the child's own awakening to his growing inner wealth. Allow and expect children to break rules. Testing is an important part of a child's development in mastering self-control. Testing limits is expected, as a child pushes back to see if this new relationship style is firmly in place. Resets provide a consistent consequence for broken rules, creating clarity around expectations and increased opportunities to create success. More importantly, resets send the meta-message that the child has it within to do what is right or expected. The reset implies greatness within. Resets are only effective after the foundation of energizing success is firmly in place. Children need to be clear that the pathway to adult intensity is through rule-following for the brief reset to hold power. When a rule is broken, parents/teachers simply and neutrally say or motion for "reset" and allow the child to correct the behavior or attitude. Resets are brief and unceremonious. The purpose is to interrupt the negative behavior and allow the child, quite literally, to reset. Resets are a separation of connection and energy and last from two seconds to a minute: only as long as it takes for the child to get back on to the success track. These are the moments of grace and forgiveness; the message to the child is one of expectation of the child's ability to tap into his greatness. We simply look for that process to begin (by the cessation of the broken rule) and reflect the success of the reset in action.

EXAMPLE:

If a child is frustrated and throws a toy at the wall, "reset" and withdraw your focus. The moment the child is not throwing (likely the next second), announce the reset success and enthusiastically energize the next moment. "Wow, you just reset. You are feeling frustrated by my answer and you are not throwing toys. You are being powerful and safe."

The power of the reset rests in the absolute clarity that negativity or misbehavior is not the pathway to adult connection. Once that is clear, through adult consistency and neutrality, this brief reset holds tremendous power to create opportunities to energize success and help a child redefine his relationship with rules.

Resets maintain a default to positivity. The interruption through reset creates the opportunity for the parent to jump to the next available moment of success. The clear message to the child is that he has it within himself to get back on the success track. The power is in the illusion that a consequence has taken place. This provides the clarity to reinforce the rules and the notion that negativity holds no value. No "punishment" is needed. When "time-in" is rich with energy and relationship, in connection with a sense of success, breaking rules pales in comparison.

Never lecture during a reset. Remain quiet, emotionally unvested and unconnected. Adults must give up emotional investment in whether or not children follow rules. When the emotional investment is high, it is nearly impossible to keep stand one in place and not give energy to the negative. As soon as the child's behavior or attitude shifts, reconnect and reflect the success. As soon as a child resets he is back in the game of time-in. Fully engage without holding a grudge about prior broken rules. It is in the past. Stay in the moment with the child, shining the light of new successes and greatness.

> NOTE: Never walk away from a child who is emotionally dysregulated and breaking rules in the context of a "meltdown." Do, however, announce the reset and begin to create and honor the successes present throughout the regulation process. By providing the clarity for rules broken and offering more adaptive behavioral choices, adults can create a success outcome that supports social learning, but does not give secondary reinforcement for misbehavior. The adult goal is to provide enough scaffolding to create a success outcome, after the clarity that comes with reset.

Might a child refuse to reset? Children will very likely refuse, as long as there continues to be adult effort to insist compliance or if the first two stands are not firmly established. This moment is a power struggle that adults must refuse to participate in. It is a moment to take stock in where one's emotional investment lies. Remember, the adult's job is not to insist on compliance, but rather to shine the light of success. This is a moment to use the emotions that well up with a child's refusal to ramp up the resolve to create success. Be aware of your own hot buttons; those offenses that create strong emotion and reaction. Often children will "refuse" reset to see what the adult reaction will be. Ironically, children will often refuse to reset while in the process of resetting. Look for the success and relentlessly go after it. Watch carefully, often children will protest while doing the very thing they were asked to do. It demonstrates great self-control to be able to do something you were asked, but do not want to do. Think of the Toll Booth Attendant and create success.

EXAMPLES:

For a child who is stomping and yelling and refusing to reset, there is a moment when they will stop to see if you are watching or to take a breath, "Wow, look at you! You are resetting yourself even though you feel disappointed by my answer to your question. You are so powerful and strong."

"Thank you for resetting. You are not arguing and that is a quality of your greatness that I appreciate."

Give children credit for resetting themselves! Resets really are two-fold. The first has to do with the cessation of breaking a rule. That part is clear; you hit and now you are not hitting, you were swearing and now you are not swearing. The second side of the reset is emotional regulation; keeping one's emotions in check and appropriate for the situation. This is a personal process and cannot be imposed. Children learn this process through experience and the support of adults calling to their attention the successful reset.

EXAMPLE:

For a child who stomps down to their room and then comes back 5 minutes later, "You are amazing! You knew just what you needed to do to reset yourself. That is a great skill."

It is important for adults to remind themselves frequently that the goal of the Nurtured Heart Approach is not better control of children, but rather children who know and feel that they have it within to control themselves. Grow this skill experientially through energizing successful resets. In fact, after stand one and two are firmly in place, and it is time to introduce the concept of reset, do so first by calling out and reflecting moments when the child, family member or classmate resets without prompting. By doing so, the concept of reset is introduced around internalized or observed success. Later, when a child is prompted to reset, he already knows that he has the capacity to do so with ease and reset is nothing to be feared.

....

There are times when a child needs more time or support to reset. For clarity purposes, it is important for the adult to announce the successful completion of a reset once it is initiated. Remember, it is not the emotion that required reset, but the broken rule. Once the behavior has stopped, announce the successful completion of the reset and give the child grace to regulate emotionally in time, with our without support.

EXAMPLE:

"You are no longer throwing things and that is powerful. Thanks for resetting. I will let you do what you need to do to feel calmer, but your reset is over."

NOTE: *For the child who has difficulty with emotional regulation, the notion of "re-setting" oneself is a necessary skill for success. This skill of emotionally resetting, when rules are not being broken, can be broken down into smaller increments, with the success being called out and energized along the continuum. It is also true that for some children, the need for a longer regulation process is not a time for adult conversation or comments. Be mindful of a child's sensory needs. This also may be a process that needs to be specifically taught through simple Cognitive-Behavioral techniques, helping children tune in to their thoughts and feelings. The beauty in the reset is that this life skill is developed experientially, as adults tune in to supporting positive efforts and creating a success outcome.*

....

If a child is having a strong emotion, but no rule has been broken, simply use an Active Recognition to reflect their emotion.

....

Recompense, restitution and reconciliation: When a child does harm to another person or property, it is reasonable to expect that child to make amends. Making amends does not mean forcing an apology, but rather, after the completion of reset, allowing the child the opportunity to make up for his offense. This should be a positive, success focused interaction, when the child is ready and with the child's active participation. Making amends is something that is done because it is the right thing to do, not as a punishment. The consequence is over with the completion of the reset. By creating the opportunity for a child to make amends successfully, we allow that child to take responsibility for his actions, to be a positive participant in the group and demonstrate ever clearer evidence of the greatness that is within.

Some children may refuse to make amends or to do the task that they were reset for refusing. It is reasonable to have a child's privileges on hold until a he makes restitution or does what was expected. This is not a punishment, rather just giving the child control to make his own good choices. Doing the right thing is guided by the heart. The moment a child completes what was required, create success around the great choices just made and how those choices reflect greatness.

....

What if the child refuses to make amends?
Remember that this is an exercise of the heart and not adult control. If a child refuses or is not ready, reflect his honesty about his emotion and extend the opportunity to collaborate or take responsibility when ready.

EXAMPLE:

"I appreciate your honesty in letting me know that you are not ready to make amends for punching a hole in the wall. That demonstrates that your apologies are not just words, but something you must feel. That is a sign of great integrity. Let me know when you are ready with ideas about how you would like to fix the wall. I'm certain that you can come up with workable options. "

"I see that you are still having big feelings and are not ready to make amends to Joey after breaking his toy. I appreciate your honesty about your feelings and I know that when you apologize it will be something that you feel and not just something that you say. That sincerity makes apologies more meaningful."

Privileges are on hold until the child has made amends, but the adult energy is one of expected success and positivity. Let the child guide the process of taking responsibility for his actions. Children will often be creative and positive in their efforts to make amends, if given the opportunity. Honor all effort to rectify the situation, even if the person offended against is not ready to receive the gesture.

EXAMPLE:

"Thank you for telling Joey that you are sorry for breaking his toy and offering to fix it. I see that he is still having big feelings and isn't ready to play, but you took responsibility and showed integrity by admitting to what you did."

When adults allow children the space to take responsibility in ways that are purposeful to them, they will often create more sincere and meaningful resolution. The moment the child makes an effort to take responsibility and make amends, create success around their gesture and the meaning behind it. Adults do not hold grudges, but move forward with greater expectation and positive energy.

EXAMPLE:

"Thanks so much for taking responsibility for putting the books back on the shelf and apologizing for throwing things. You could have refused, but you came back and took care of the mess that you created. That shows great maturity and self-control and those are qualities of your greatness that I admire."

Tips for Success!

- Safety comes first! Be certain that a child's behavior is not a safety concern and react appropriately if it is.

- Relationship is not an option. It is impossible not to be in a relationship with a child in your care, but you can choose to make this relationship one based on success.

- Trust that resistance is part of the change process. Behaviors may get worse before they get better. As children push back, use this intensity to increase your resolve for creating success.

- Power is NOT in punishment; power is in growing inner wealth.

- Celebrate everyday moments through the creation of successes.

- As soon as you put your energy into something, you will see more of it.

- Social communication is always ON—you are always sending a message, so choose it carefully.

- Refuse to talk about problems—talking about problems grows more problems.

- Be mindful that the Nurtured Heart Approach is your process, not your child's.

- Be ready! Once you begin the Nurtured Heart journey, all of your relationships will begin to change.

- Enjoy the feeling of experiencing a child stand in his greatness!

Greatness-Growing Vocabulary

Reflect on a child's Greatness in each opportunity-filled moment. Rather than "thank you" or "good job," choose to create meaningful and contextual moments of success by accusing a child, in the moment, of being the Greatness quality of...

Joyful **Considerate** Attentive Cooperative **A hard worker** A source of strength

Courageous A leader **Constructive** **A helper** Committed Creative **A great example**

Courteous An advocate **Aware** Dedicated to success Diligent Discerning **Direct**

Accomplished a lot Creative Dignified Appreciative **Easy to like** Deeply understanding

A good friend **Attentive to detail** Productive **Demonstrating integrity** Exceeding expectations

Gentle **Inspiring** Surprising **Efficient** Empathetic Powerful Wise Faithful **Brave**

Focused Bringing out the best in others Forgiving **Generous** Choosing what's important

Compassionate Gracious **Going above and beyond** **Humility** **Honest** Peacekeeper

Genuine **Glorious** Productive Good-hearted Reasonable Respectful **Having unique**

ideas Resourceful Energetic **Responsible** **Respecting self** Reliable **Enthusiastic**

Having great curiosity **Thankful** **Self-controlled** Handling strong emotions well **Inspiring**

Seeing the big picture Having an open mind Honorable Having a positive attitude

Strong on the inside Hopeful Trustworthy **Independent** Thoughtful **Inquisitive**

Understanding Intelligent **Just and fair** Kind Loving **Using a pleasant voice**

Using his great mind **Vibrant** Visionary **Looking out for others** Managing time well

A quick mind Making great choices **Brilliant thoughts** Making a great guess

Organized Patient **A great sense of humor** Logical Pulling together

Amazing forethought **Enthusiastic** Excellent planning skills Teamwork

Modest Tenacious Responsible **Deliberate** Showing character Growing Greatness

Draw Or Write About Your Own Greatness

CPSIA information can be obtained at www.ICGtesting.com
Printed in the USA
BVOW100059200613

323807BV00003B/11/P